Journeys

Direct Instruction Reading

Level 1

Textbook 1

Siegfried Engelmann
Owen Engelmann
Karen Lou Seitz Davis

A Division of The McGraw·Hill Companies

Columbus, Ohio

Illustration Credits

Shirley Beckes, Cynthia Brodie, Dan Clifford, Olivia Cole, Mark Corcoran, Simon Galkin, Dara Goldman, Meryl Henderson, Gay W. Holland, John Edwards and Associates, Susan Jerde, Anne Kennedy, Pat Lucas-Morris, Loretta Lustig, Jim Shough, Charlie Shaw, and Lauren Simeone.

SRA/McGraw-Hill

A Division of The **McGraw·Hill** *Companies*

Copyright © 2000 by SRA/McGraw-Hill. All rights reserved. Except as permitted under the United States Copyright Act, no part of this publication may be reproduced or distributed in any form or by any means, or stored in a database or retrieval system, without prior written permission from the publisher.

Printed in the United States of America.

Send all inquiries to:
SRA/McGraw-Hill
8787 Orion Place
Columbus, OH 43240-4027

ISBN 0-02-683515-0

2 3 4 5 6 7 8 9 VHJ 03 02 01 00

 m s n **1**

o a f t r ee

ai   ea

1. <u>man</u>
2. <u>see</u>
3. <u>no</u>

1. <u>m**e**an</u>
2. <u>ra**i**n</u>
3. <u>ma**i**l</u>

1. see
2. no
3. man

y s i f y e

4

1. <u>my</u>
2. <u>try</u>
3. <u>fly</u>

1. <u>eat</u>
2. <u>neat</u>
3. <u>sail</u>

e a o

1. <u>I</u> <u>am</u> <u>Sam</u>.
2. <u>at</u> <u>me</u>
3. <u>I</u> <u>see</u> <u>a</u> <u>man</u>.

1. I eat.
2. I eat a loaf.
3. I sat.

a.

b.

c.

d.

e.

1. I see foam fly.
2. I am a seal.

a.

b.

c.

d.

e.

f.

1. I see a tan fly.
2. I feel a fly.

 a f s n y r 8

1. my
2. no
3. for
4. man

1. lo<u>a</u>n
2. n<u>ai</u>l
3. m<u>e</u><u>a</u>l

a.

b.

c.

d.

e.

18

1. I see my meal.
2. I am no meal for a man.

9

m l ea r p

1. e<u>a</u>r
2. n<u>ea</u>r
3. an
4. ran

1. n<u>ai</u>l
2. l<u>oa</u>n
3. s<u>ea</u>t

a.
b.
c.
d.
e.

1. See my s<u>ea</u>t.
2. L<u>oa</u>n me a n<u>ai</u>l.

See my s<u>ea</u>t.

L<u>oa</u>n me a n<u>ai</u>l.

1. <u>I</u> <u>see</u> <u>no</u> <u>ant</u>.
2. <u>I</u> <u>feel</u> <u>an</u> <u>ant</u>.

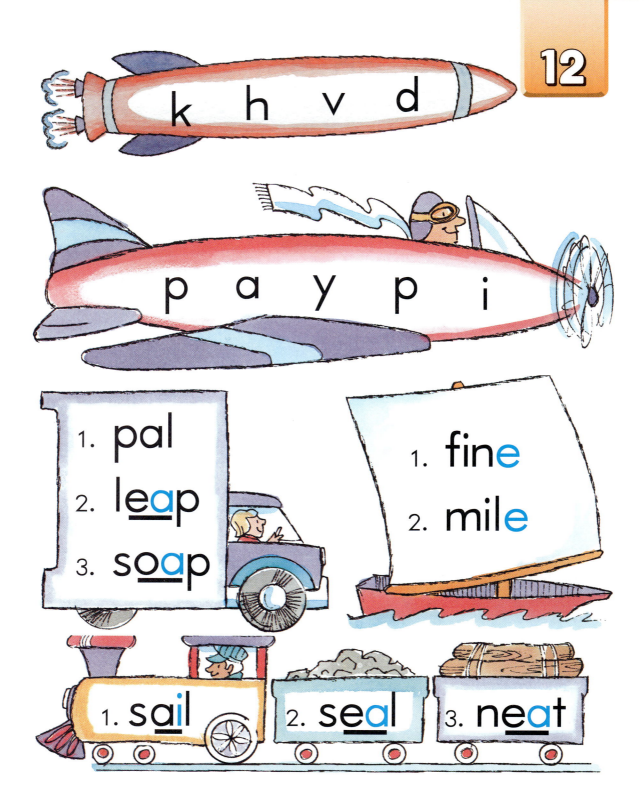

1. See me sail.
2. I am a seal.

See me sail.

13

1. I am no ram.
2. See my pal eat.

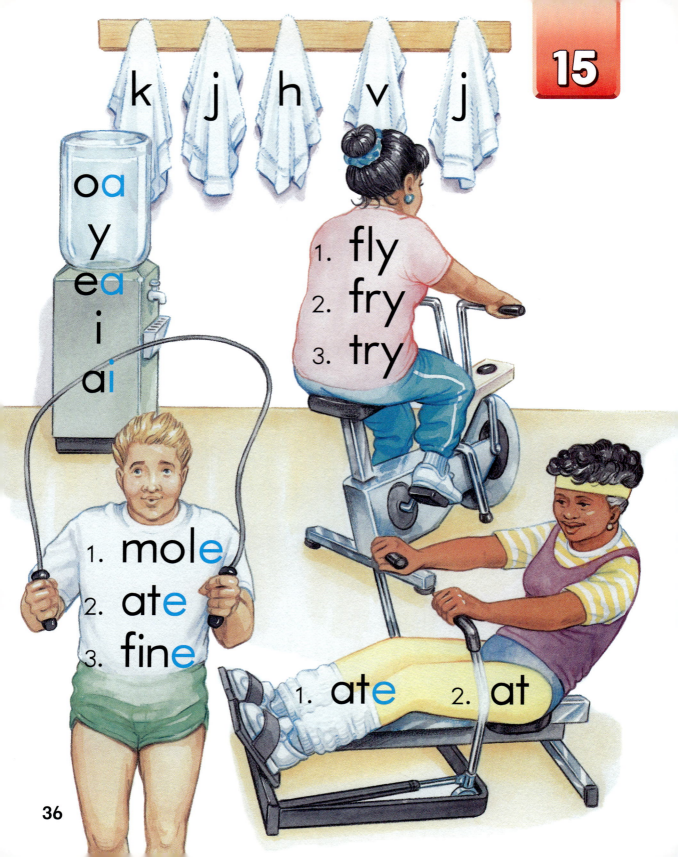

15

1. I am near my pal.
2. I am near a ram.

1

I am near my pal.

37

16

j k c h c k

ai p oa t ea y

1. at
2. sat
3. rat

1. pan
2. tan
3. near
4. mail

1. sore 2. name
3. time

1. A ram ran at me.
2. I ran at a ram.

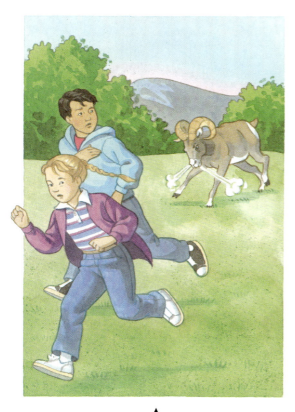

1. A ram ran at me.
2. I ran at a ram.

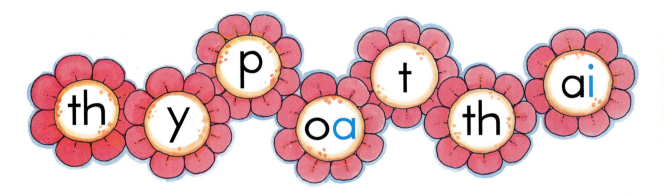

1. e_ar_
2. an
3. or
4. feet

1. sat 2. saf e
3. at e 4. at

41

1. I am safe.
2. My feet feel fine.

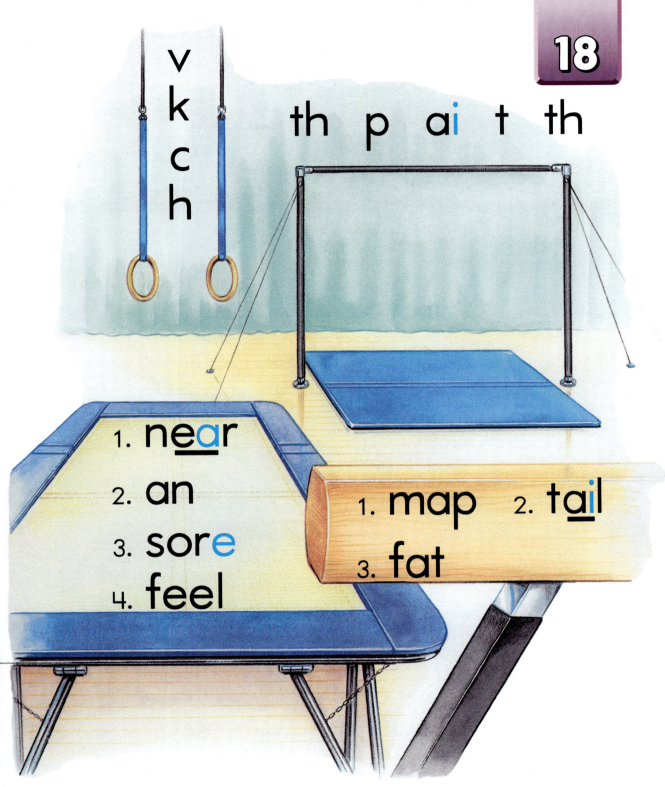

1. I feel rain.
2. My feet feel fine.

☆ c ☆ w ☆ d ☆ w ☆ v **19**

y i th ai p t th

1. fly
2. ne<u>a</u>r
3. feet
4. sat

1. pal
2. p<u>ai</u>l
3. pile

1. Sam
2. same
3. name
4. more

45

1. A fly sat near me.
2. My feet feel sore.

1. I am a fly.
2. I fly near an ear.

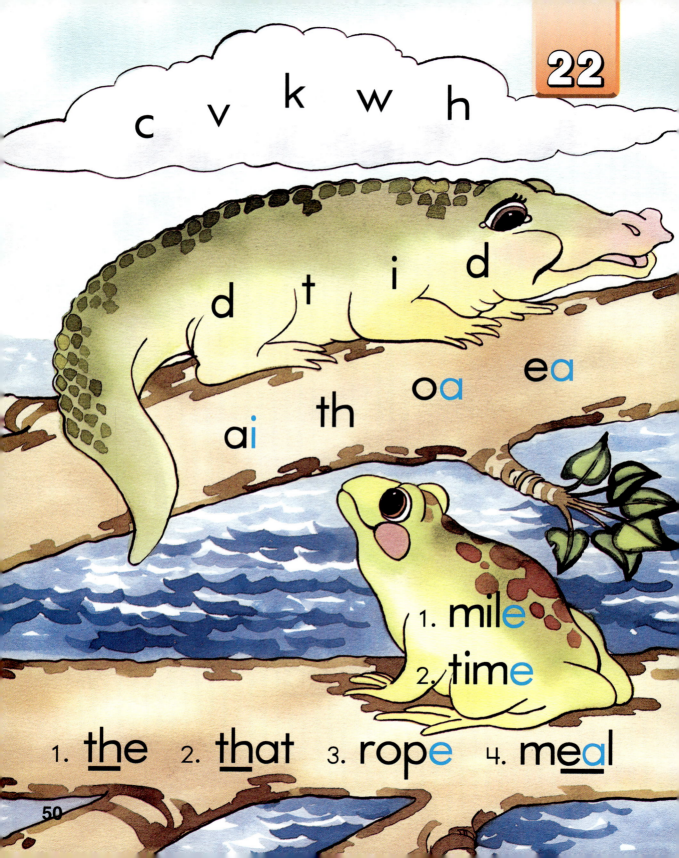

1. I rope a ram.
2. See my pal fly.

w n g h g v

p d t d

1. n<u>e</u><u>a</u>r
2. t<u>e</u><u>a</u>r
3. m<u>e</u><u>a</u>l

an
man

1. fin<u>e</u>
2. pil<u>e</u>
3. rop<u>e</u>

1. I see a man fly.
2. I eat a meal.

The ram ran at the man. So that man ran for a mile.

The ram ran at the man.

So that man ran for a mile.

A rat ran at a mole. So that mole ran near a pile.

A rat ran at a mole.

So that mole ran near a pile.

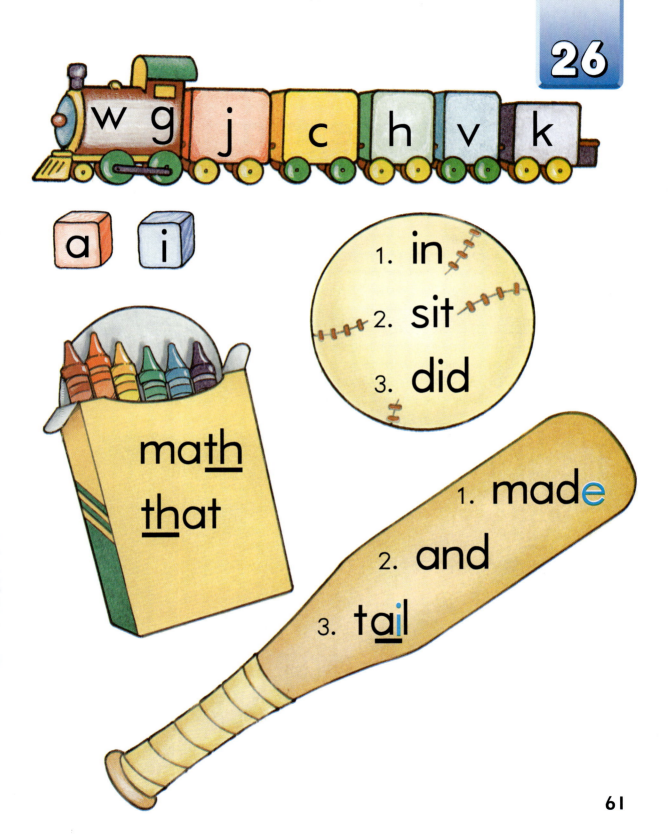

I sat near a tail. I made a rope.

I sat near a tail.

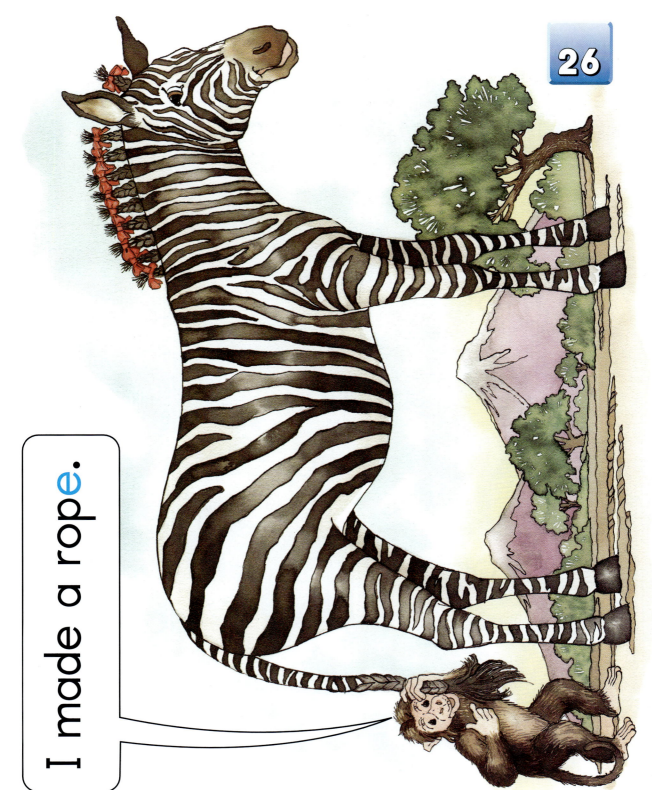

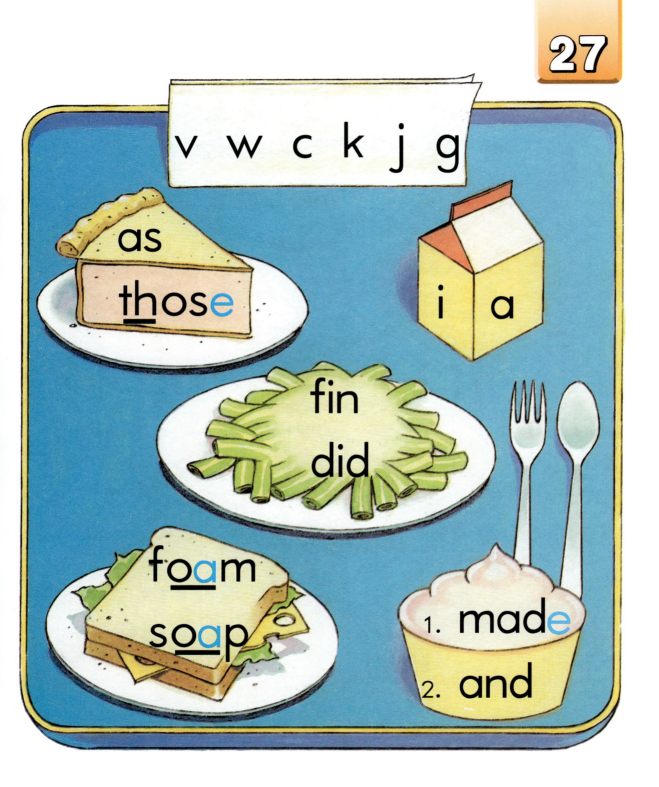

I see foam and a tail. I see no soap near me.

I see foam and a tail.

A mole made a pile.
That pile made the ram mad.

A mole made a pile.

That pile made the ram mad.

I sit near my pal. That pal is my dad.

It is time for the mail. That mail is for me. My soap is in that mail.

The rain made a ram sit. So that ram is mad.

The rain made me sit.

My soap is in the mail. Rain made that soap foam. An ant is in the foam.

My soap is in the mail.

Rain made that soap foam.

An ant is in the foam.

A seal and a ram may play. Or the seal may sleep. And the ram may eat a sail.

A seal may sleep.

A ram may eat a sail.

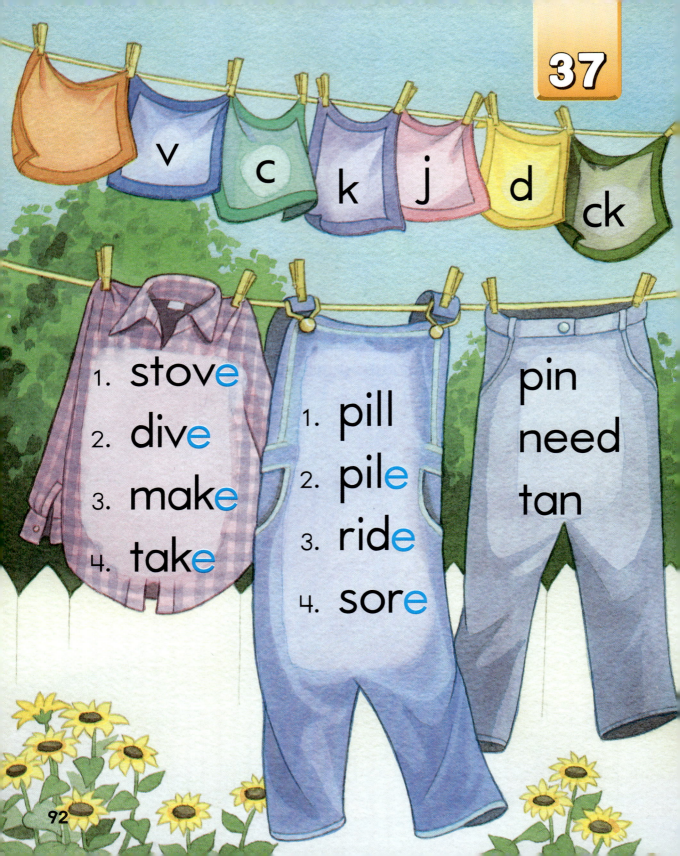

I see rain. My pal may play in the rain. Or my pal may eat.

I see rain.

My pal m<u>a</u>y pl<u>a</u>y in t<u>h</u>e r<u>ai</u>n.

Or my pal may eat.

I like my pal. My pal may take me for a ride. That may make me sore.

I like my pal.

My pal may take me for a ride.

That may make me sore.

39

An ant is in a pine tree.

Is that ant safe?

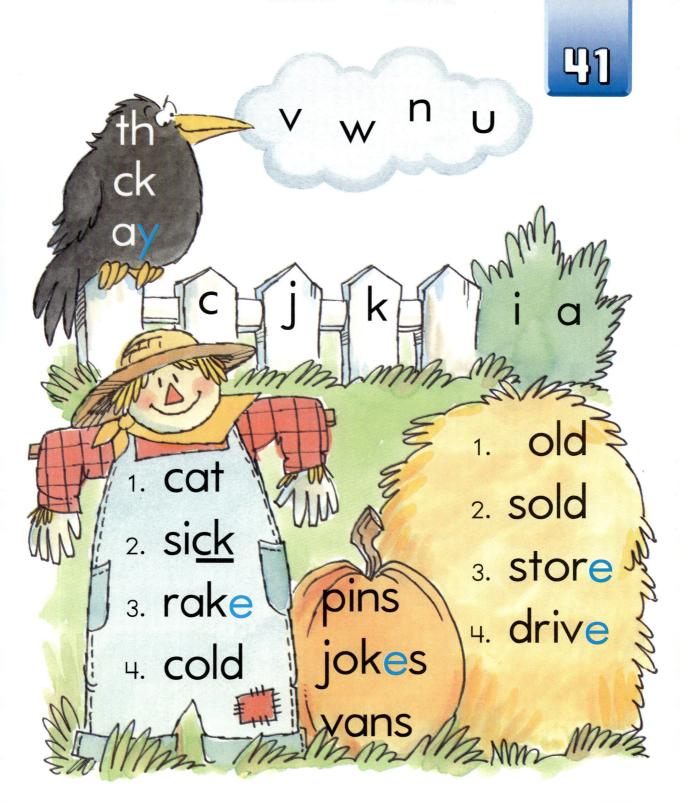

An ant is in a van. Is a man in <u>th</u>at van? No. See a mole drive.

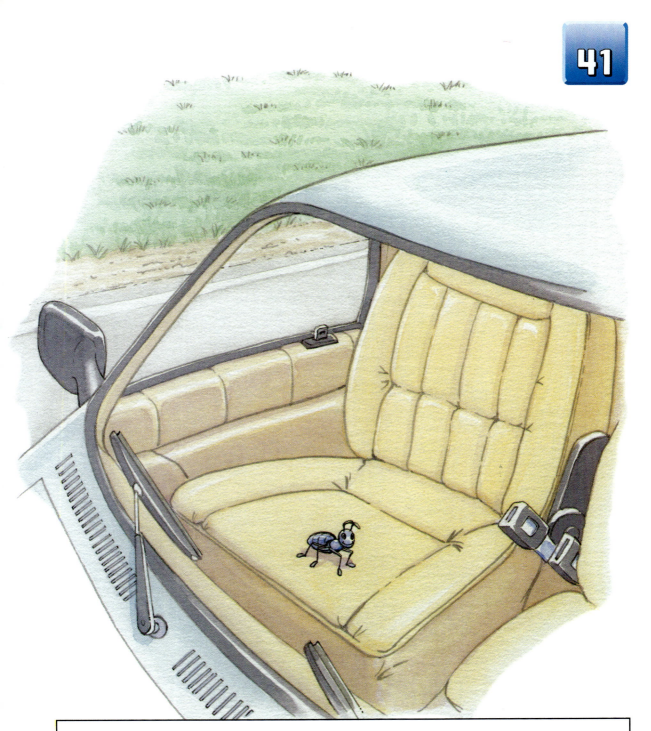

An ant is in a van.

Is a man in t̲h̲e̲ van?
No. See a mole drive.

Is a rat near the lake?
No. Is the rat in this
tree? No. Is that rat
in a store?

Is a rat near the lake?

Is the rat in this tree?

That rat is in a store.

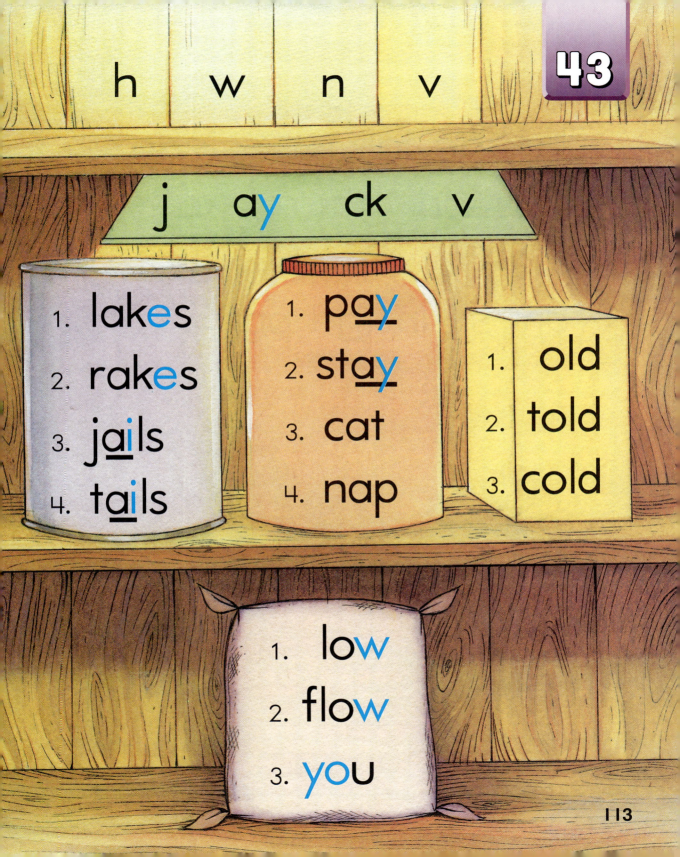

Did the tan ram sleep?
No. Did that ram dive in
a lake? No. Did that
ram sit in the path? No.

Did the tan ram sleep?

Did that ram dive in a lake?

Did the tan ram sit in the path?

A seal and 3 pals sat near a lake. Those pals may play in the lake. Or those pals may take a nap.

A seal and 3 pals sat near a lake.

Those pals may play in the lake.

Or those pals may take a nap.

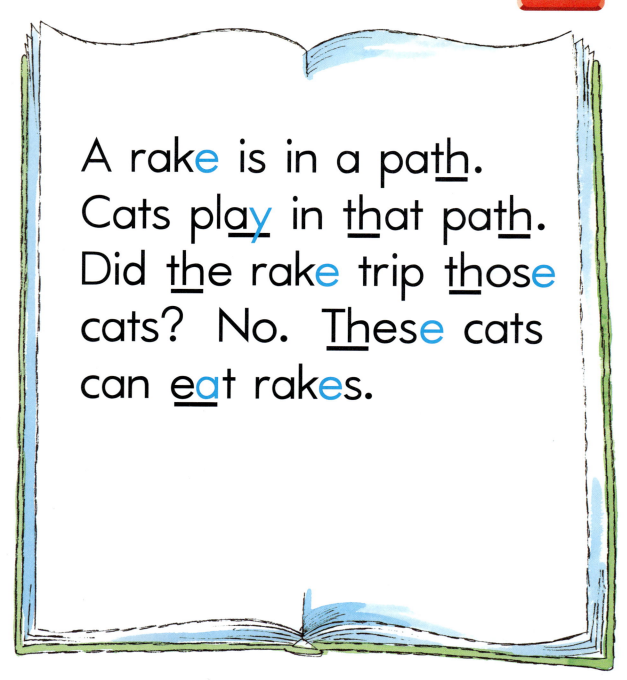

A rake is in a path. Cats play in that path. Did the rake trip those cats? No. These cats can eat rakes.

A rake is in a path.

Cats play in that path.

Did the rake trip those cats? No. These cats can eat rakes.

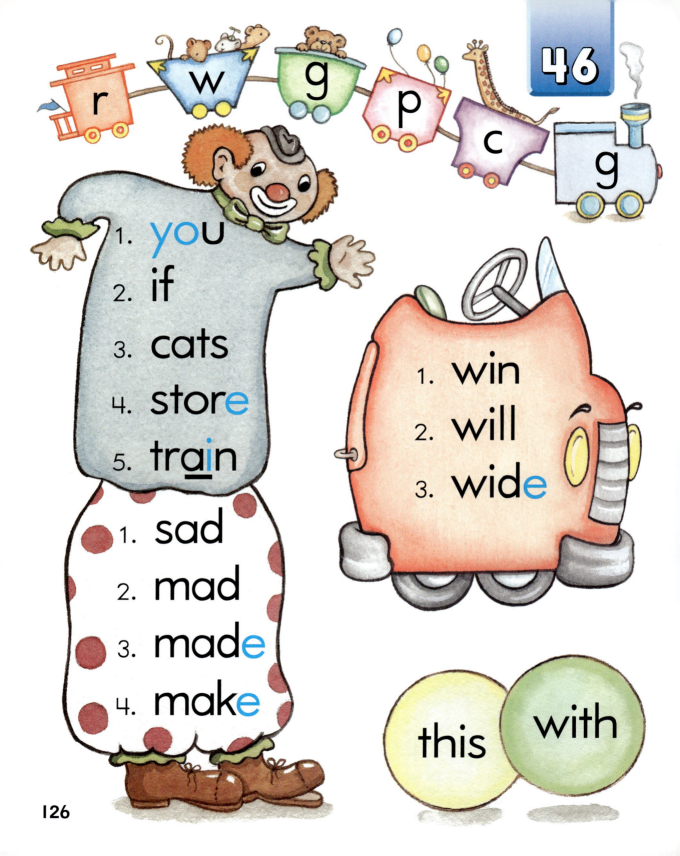

A man is near a lake.
A cat will trip that man.
Will make the man mad? You will see.

A man is near a lake.

A cat will trip that man.

That made the man mad.

Cats ran in a store. A man made those cats sit. Did that make the cats mad? You will see.

Cats ran in a store.

A man made those cats sit. Did that make the cats mad?

48

1. needs
2. seeds
3. rak**e**s
4. mak**e**s

w   g   c

1. s**a**id
2. ov**e**r
3. sno**w**
4. deep
5. we

1. s**e**als
2. cold
3. fiv**e**
4. tr**a**ils
5. tr**a**ins

133

A ram sat in the snow. That snow made the ram feel cold. The ram told five seals that the snow is cold. Did that make the seals mad? No. Those seals like cold snow.

A ram sat in the snow. That snow made the ram feel cold.

Did that make the seals mad? No.

It is a cold d<u>ay</u>. Snow is in the stove. A cat and a rat feel cold. Is an ant as cold as the stove? No. That ant is in five c<u>oa</u>ts.

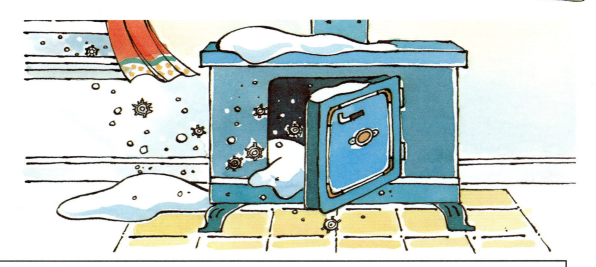

It is a cold d<u>ay</u>. Snow is in the stove.

A cat and a rat feel cold. Is an ant as cold as the stove?

No. That ant is in five coats.